True or False?

Colours

Daniel Nunn

Raintree

Raintree is an imprint of Capstone Global Library
Limited, a company incorporated in England and Wales
having its registered office at 7 Pilgrim Street, London,
EC4V 6LB – Registered company number: 6695582

To contact Raintree please phone 0845 6044371,
fax + 44 (0) 1865 312263,
or email myorders@raintreepublishers.co.uk.
Customers from outside the UK please telephone
+44 1865 312262.

Text © Capstone Global Library Limited 2013
First published in hardback in 2013
The moral rights of the proprietor have been asserted.

Edited by Dan Nunn, Rebecca Rissman,
and Catherine Veitch
Designed by Joanna Hinton-Malivoire
Picture research by Ruth Blair
Production by Victoria Fitzgerald
Originated by Capstone Global Library
Printed and bound in China by Leo Paper Products
Limited

ISBN 978 1 406 25155 5
16 15 14 13 12
10 9 8 7 6 5 4 3 2 1

British Library Cataloguing in Publication Data
Nunn, Daniel.
Colours. – (True or false?)
535.6-dc23
A full catalogue record for this book is available from
the British Library.

Acknowledgements
We would like to thank the following for permission to
reproduce photographs: iStockphoto p. 10 (© William
Randall); Shutterstock pp. 4 (© Leigh Prather), 5 and
back cover (© Maks Narodenko), 6 (© AnnaDe), 7
and back cover (© Le Do), 8 (© Oleg Znamenskiy), 9
(© Christophe Testi), 11 (© Richard Peterson), 12 (©
Johan W. Elzenga), 13 (© Andresr), 14 (© Andresr), 15
(© tarasov), 16 (© Thomas Klee), 18 (© neelsky), 17 (©
Anan Kaewkhammul), 19 (© luckyraccoon), 20 (© Eric
Gevaert), 22 (© Pichugin Dmitry).

Cover photograph of an elephant reproduced with
permission of Shutterstock (© Richard Peterson).

Every effort has been made to contact copyright holders
of material reproduced in this book. Any omissions will
be rectified in subsequent printings if notice is given to
the publisher.

Contents

Colours

Colours are all around us. How much do **YOU** know about colours?

Bananas

Bananas are purple.

 **True or false?**

5

✖ False!

Bananas are not purple.
Bananas are yellow.

Flamingos

Flamingos are pink.

 **True** or **false?**

7

✔ True!

Flamingos are pink. Flamingos turn pink from the food they eat!

Fire engines

Fire engines are blue.

 **True or false?**

9

✖ False!

Fire engines are not blue. Most fire engines are red.

Elephants

Elephants
are green.

 **True or false?**

11

✖ False!

Elephants are not green.
Elephants are grey!

12

Traffic lights

The red light on a traffic light means "Go!"

 **True or false?**

13

STOP!

GO!

✕ **False!**

The red light means "Stop!" The green light means "Go!"

Tomatoes

Tomatoes come in different colours.

 **True or false?**

✔ True!

Tomatoes come in different colours. Tomatoes can be red, yellow, orange, or green.

Tigers

Tigers have black and orange stripes.

 **True or false?**

17

✔ True!

Tigers have black and orange stripes.
The stripes help them to hide.

Zebras

Zebras have black and orange stripes, too!

 **True or false?**

✖ False!

Zebras do not have black and orange stripes. Zebras have black and white stripes.

Rainbows

The colours of a rainbow are black, red, white, purple, green, orange, grey, and pink.

 **True or false?**

✗ False!

Those are not the colours. The colours of the rainbow are red, orange, yellow, green, blue, indigo, and violet.

Can you remember?

Which animal is pink?

What colour is a zebra?

What colour is a fire engine?

Look back through the book to check your answers.

Index

Activity

Make your own True or False game

Help your child to make their own Colours: True or False game. Collect a selection of pictures from magazines and postcards. Mount each picture on card. Then with the child write a series of true or false statements about the colour of things in the pictures on separate pieces of card. Put one statement with each corresponding picture. On the back of each picture write if the statement is true or false. For the game, read the statement out loud, ask the child if it is true or false, then turn over the picture to see if the child is correct. To extend the activity, ask the child to write the statements and whether they are true or false, and then ask you the questions.

599

JEWISH

2 WEEK LOAN

This item is to be returned to the library on or before the last date stamped below.

Leeds City College

BE ☑ EN ☐ HF ☐ PL ☐ PW ☐ TC ☐

Renew on 0113

216 2046   or   284 6246   or   386 1705

www.lcc-library.appspot.com